# Crochet Botanicals

Kati Gàlusz

chartwell
books

# Quarto

© 2024 Quarto Publishing Group USA Inc.

This edition published in 2024 by Chartwell Books,
an imprint of The Quarto Group
142 West 36th Street, 4th Floor
New York, NY 10018 USA
T (212) 779-4972 F (212) 779-6058
www.Quarto.com

10 9 8 7 6 5 4 3 2

Chartwell titles are also available at discount for retail, wholesale, promotional, and bulk purchase. For details, contact the Special Sales Manager by email at specialsales@quarto.com or by mail at The Quarto Group, Attn: Special Sales Manager, 100 Cummings Center Suite 265D, Beverly, MA 01915, USA.

ISBN: 978-0-7858-4481-5

Publisher: Wendy Friedman
Senior Publishing Manager: Meredith Mennitt
Cover Design: Kate Sinclair
Designer: Angelika Piwowarczyk
Editor: Meredith Mennitt
Author: Katalin Gálusz

All stock design elements ©Shutterstock

Printed in China

# Table of Contents

# About This Kit

This kit contains the tools and materials you will need to make your own crochet flowers: yarn in green, yellow, white, pink, blue and brown; a G/6 (4mm) crochet hook; yarn needle; two brooch pin backings; embroidery floss and sewing needle.

If using colors as written, you will have enough yarn to make at least one of each design except for the red poppy.

## HOW TO READ THE INSTRUCTIONS

Every line starts with the round/row number in bold, and ends with the stitch count in parentheses.

Instructions in square brackets must be repeated the specified number of times before continuing with the remaining instructions of the round or row (if any).

# Abbreviations

**BL** ～～～～ back loop

**ch** ～～～～ chain or chains

**dc** ～～～～ double crochet

**FL** ～～～～ front loop

**rnd** ～～～～ round

**sc** ～～～～ single crochet

**sl st** ～～～～ slip stitch

**st** ～～～～ stitch or stitches

**tr** ～～～～ treble crochet

**YO** ～～～～ yarn over

# Tools & Materials

The flower on the left was made with light worsted acrylic and 4mm hook, the one on the right with cotton thread and 1.25mm hook

## YARN

The patterns in this kit were designed with light worsted acrylic yarn, but don't let that limit you—they would work just as well with other materials and yarn weights! Super bulky chenille yarn would give you big, cuddly flowers, while crochet thread would make small, elegant pieces perfect to create jewelry.

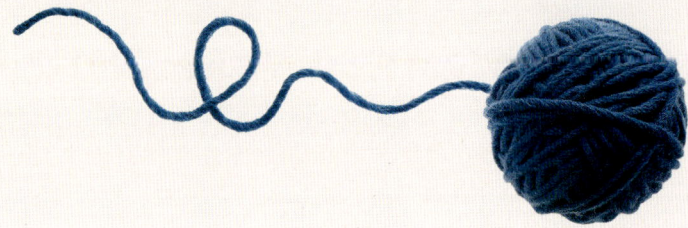

## HOOK SIZE AND GAUGE

The sample projects in this kit were made with a G/6 (4mm) hook, but if you use different materials, you will have to match your hook size to the yarn. Exact gauge is not important, as long as the crocheted fabric you create is firm and dense—a good starting point is a hook 1 or 2 sizes smaller hook than what's recommended on the yarn label.

Note: the finished sizes of the flowers listed in the patterns apply to flowers made with light worsted yarn and 4mm hook.

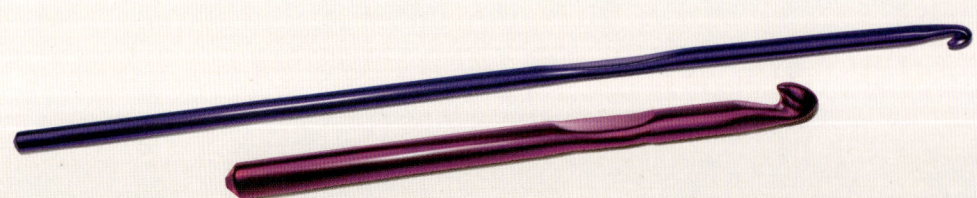

## STITCH MARKER

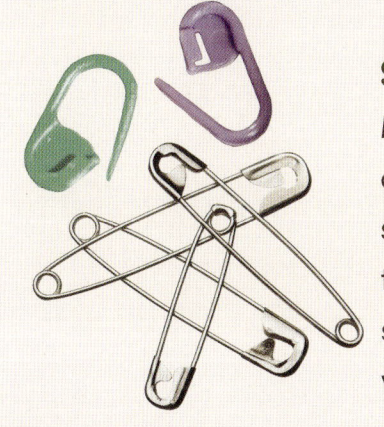

Most of these flowers have rounds that are easy to keep track of, but you might need to use a marker for the center of the sunflower: insert it into the first stitch of the round, moving it to the next round when you start it. There are special locking or split ring markers for crochet, but a safety pin or a paper clip will work just as well.

## NEEDLES

Except for the rose and the poppy, the patterns in this kit can be completed without sewing. But depending on what you plan to use the flowers for, a large yarn needle might be still necessary to weave in yarn ends, or to sew appliques to a crocheted/knit fabric.

A regular sewing needle, with thread or embroidery floss, can be used to attach flowers to brooch pins, hair clips, etc., as well as to sew on optional decorations such as beads.

## EMBROIDERY FLOSS

Embroidery floss is loosely spun from six individual strands, and can be used as is or split into separate threads. When sewing crochet pieces on metal parts, 1 or 2 strands of floss with a small sharp needle will allow you finer stitches and more control than you would have with yarn.

# Stitches & Techniques

This chapter contains a short primer on the techniques you will need to create the flowers, but if you are new to crochet, I suggest practicing the basics first. Many yarn shops offer classes, or you can look up video tutorials online.

## Slip knot

Use this to begin a chain. Make a loop on your yarn a few inches from the end. **(FIG. A)** Insert your hook through the loop and grab the yarn end connected to the skein. Pull the strand through the loop, then tighten the knot. **(FIG. B)**

**FIG. A**

**FIG. B**

## Yarn Over (YO)

Wrap the yarn around your hook from back to front.

## Chain (ch)

Make a slip knot first, unless you are in the middle of a piece and already have a loop on your hook. YO, and pull yarn through the loop on hook. **(FIG. C)** Repeat as many times as required.

The loop on the hook doesn't count as chain, so omit it if you are checking the stitch count.

**FIG. C**

**FIG. D**

## Working into Chains

Usually, you must skip the ch nearest to the hook and work your first st in the 2nd or 3rd ch from hook (the pattern will always specify this).

When you look at a row of chains, the front side will look like a series of tiny Vs, and the back will have a single line of bumps. **(FIG. D)** When symmetry is especially important, insert your hook into these back bumps rather than one of the front strands.

## Working into a Ring

Rather than inserting your hook into the individual chains themselves, insert it through the center of the ring or space created by the whole chain.

## Working into Stitches

Every stitch has two strands in a small V shape on top. Insert your hook under both loops of the V unless otherwise specified.

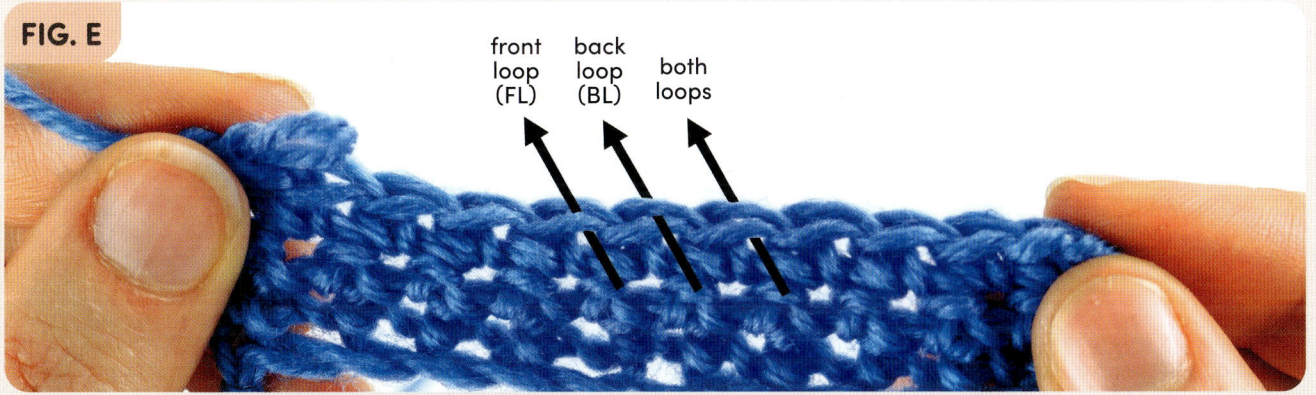

FIG. E

front loop (FL)  back loop (BL)  both loops

## Working in Back Loop (BL)/Front Loop (FL)

When you look at the V on top of the stitch, the strand closest to you is called the front loop and the strand farthest from you is called the back loop. If you need to work in BL, insert your hook under the farthest loop only. If you need to work in FL, insert your hook under the closest loop only. **(FIG. E)**

## Slip Stitch (sl st)

Insert your hook into the st or ch, YO and pull yarn through both the st or ch and the loop on hook. **(FIG. F)** Be careful to keep the stitch loose: the V on top should be the same size as the top of other stitches.

FIG. F

**FIG. G**

## Single Crochet (sc)

This is the stitch you will use most for amigurumi. Insert your hook into the st or ch, YO and draw up a loop (pull yarn through st or ch). You will have 2 loops on your hook. YO and pull yarn through both loops on hook. **(FIG. G)**

## Double Crochet (dc)

YO, insert your hook in st or ch, YO and draw up a loop (3 loops on hook). YO and draw yarn through 2 loops on hook, then YO again and pull through the remaining 2 loops on hook.

## Treble Crochet (tr)

YO twice, insert your hook into the st or ch, YO, and draw up a loop (4 loops on hook). *YO and pull through 2 loops on hook, then repeat from * twice more.

## Fastening Off

Cut the yarn 2–3 inches from your hook (or more, if you will need the yarn end for sewing), YO and pull the end through the last loop on the hook.

For some designs, a different method is preferable: after cutting the yarn, pull on the last loop on your hook until the yarn end is drawn through. The pattern will always specify which method to use.

## Dealing with Yarn Ends

After fastening off, pull the yarn end to the back of the flower either with your hook or with a yarn needle.

If the backside will be invisible, you can tie the starting and ending yarn tails together to secure them, then either keep them for sewing, or trim them short if you won't need them.

If the flower's back will be visible, you must weave in the ends by sewing them through several stitches, then snip off the rest as close to the crochet fabric as possible.

## Joining a New Color

Insert your hook into the specified st or ch, YO and pull up a loop, then ch 1. This chain does not count as a chain of the pattern.

## Magic Ring

The magic ring, sometimes called adjustable ring, is a nice technique to start working in the round, because it will create a small circle of stitches with no gap in the center.

Make a circle in the yarn to form a ring, insert hook through this ring, YO and draw up a loop, then ch 1. Work the first round of stitches over both the ring and the free yarn end, then pull on the free end (tail) to close the ring.

## Right and Wrong Side

For all these flowers, the right side is the side facing you while you crochet.

# Patterns

# 1. Simple Flowers

## A: Small Flower

**Finished size: 7/8" diameter**

**Rnd 1:** with white, make a slip knot. Ch 4 and sl st in the 4th ch from hook (**FIG. A, B**), [ch 3 and sl st in the same ch] 4 times (**FIG. C, D, E**) (5 petals made)

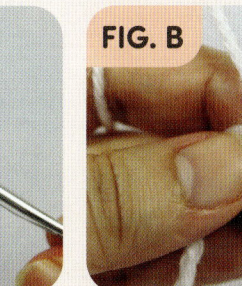

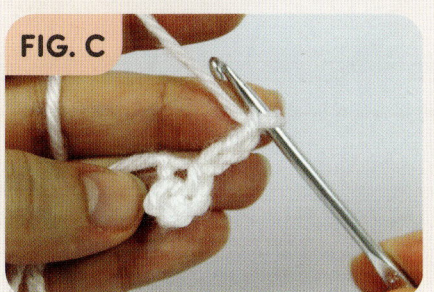

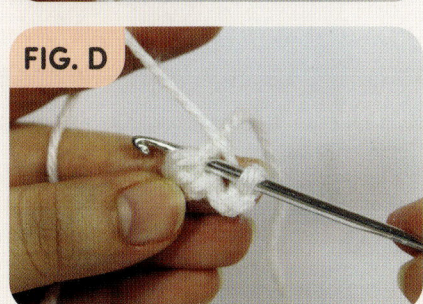

Cut the yarn and pull on the last loop until you draw the end through (**FIG. E**). Bring the yarn end to the back through the flower's center (**FIG. F**), then tie it together with the starting tail (**FIG. G**).

## B: Medium Flower; Finished size: 1 1/8" diameter

**Rnd 1:** With white, make a slip knot. Ch 3, dc in the 3rd ch from hook, ch 2 and sl st in the same ch. **(FIG. A)** [Ch 2, dc in the same ch, ch 2 and sl st in the same ch] 4 times **(FIG. B, C, D, E)** (5 petals made)

Cut the yarn and pull on the last loop until you draw the end through.

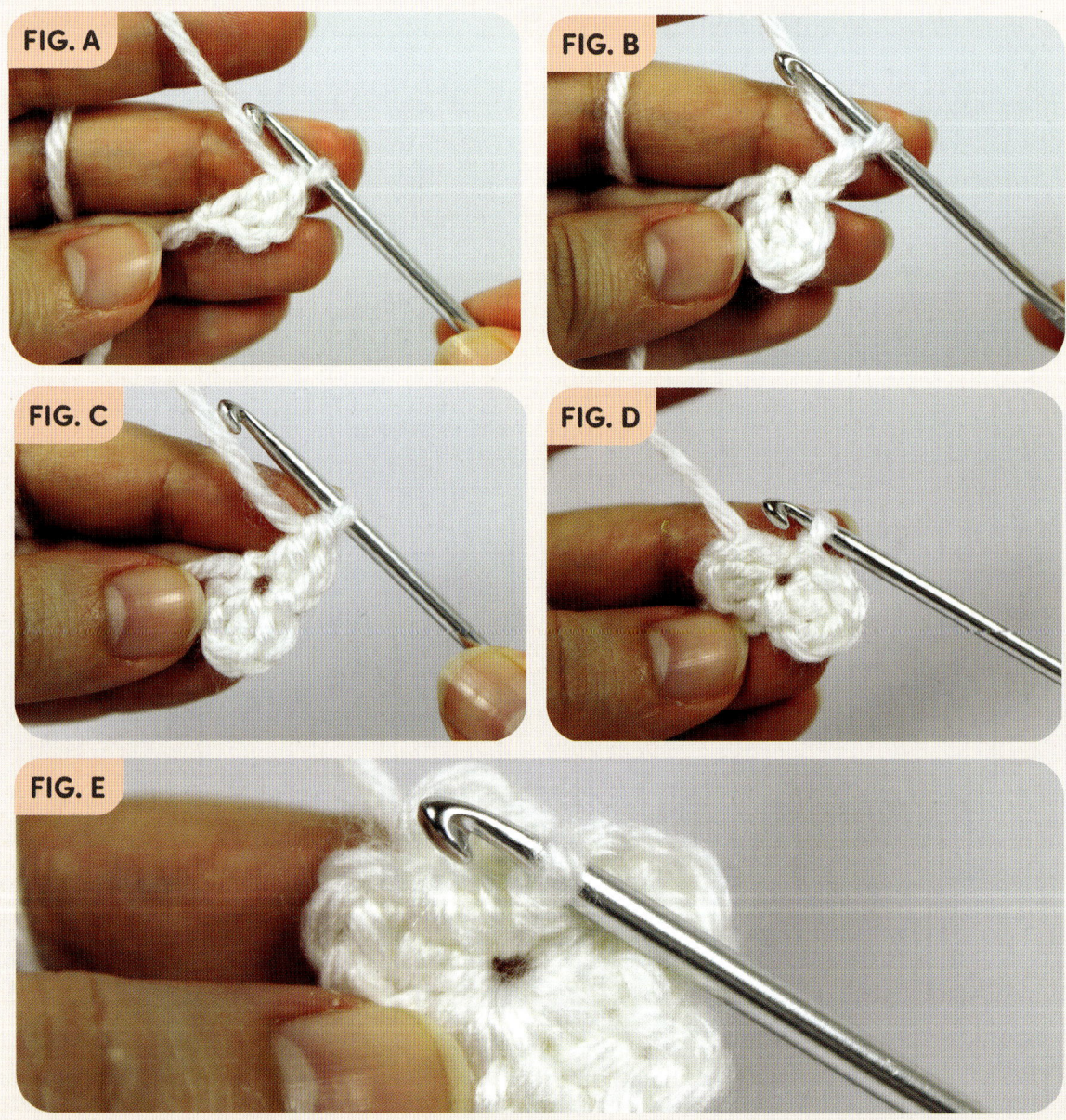

FIG. A
FIG. B
FIG. C
FIG. D
FIG. E

Bring the yarn end to the back through the flower's center, then tie it together with the starting tail (See **FIG. F** and **G** on p. 15).

## C: Large Flower; Finished size: 1 3/8" diameter

**Rnd 1:** With white, make a slip knot. Ch 4 and sl st in the 1st ch you made to join the chains in a ring. **(FIG. A)** Sc 5 into the ring **(FIG. B)** (5sc)

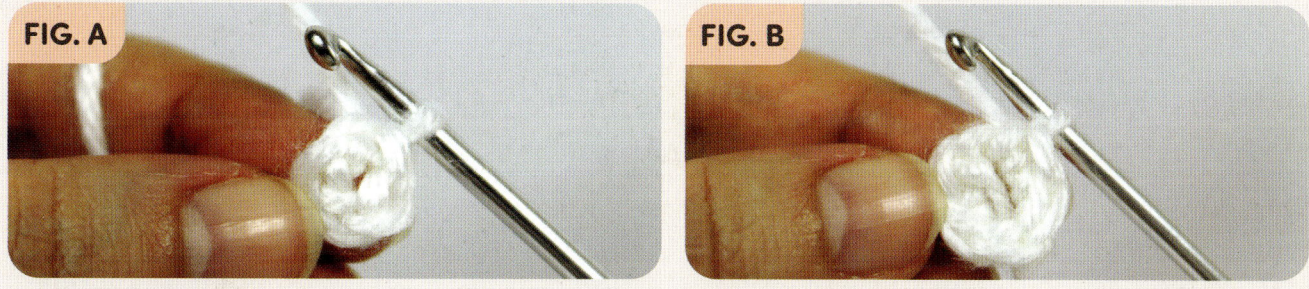

FIG. A

FIG. B

**Rnd 2:** [sl st into the next st, ch 2, dc 2 into the same st, ch 2] 5 times **(FIG. C, D, E, F, G)** (5 petals made)

FIG. C

FIG. D

FIG. E

FIG. F

FIG. G

Sl st into the next st (the first sl st of rnd 2) **(FIG. H)**. Cut the yarn and pull on the last loop until you draw the end through. Bring the yarn end to the back through the same st **(FIG. I)**, then tie it together with the starting tail **(FIG. J)**.

FIG. H

FIG. I

FIG. J

# 2. Two-Layer Flower

**Finished size: 2 3/4" diameter**

**Rnd 1:** With yellow yarn, make a slip knot. Ch 4, dc in the 4th ch from hook **(FIG. A)**, then dc 8 more into the same ch **(FIG. B)**. Sl st to the top of the 4-ch column **(FIG. C)** (9 dc plus the ch-column)

**Rnd 2:** [ch 4, skip 1 st, sl st in the BL of the next st **(FIG. D, E, F)**] 5 times (5 chain loops made) **(FIG. G)**

Cut yarn, YO and pull the end through the last loop on hook.

In the next round, ignore the chain loops you just made (fold them back to get them out of the way) and work into the stitches of rnd 1.

**Rnd 3:** Join white into any unworked st of rnd 1 **(FIG. H)**. [Ch 1, work 4 dc in the FL of the next st **(FIG. I, J)**, ch 1 and sl st in both loops of the next st **(FIG. K)**] 5 times (5 petals made) **(FIG. L)**

Cut the yarn and pull on the last loop until you draw the end through. Bring the yarn end to the back through the same st.

Fold the petals you just made forward to reveal the chain loops from rnd 2, work the next round into these loops **(FIG. M)**.

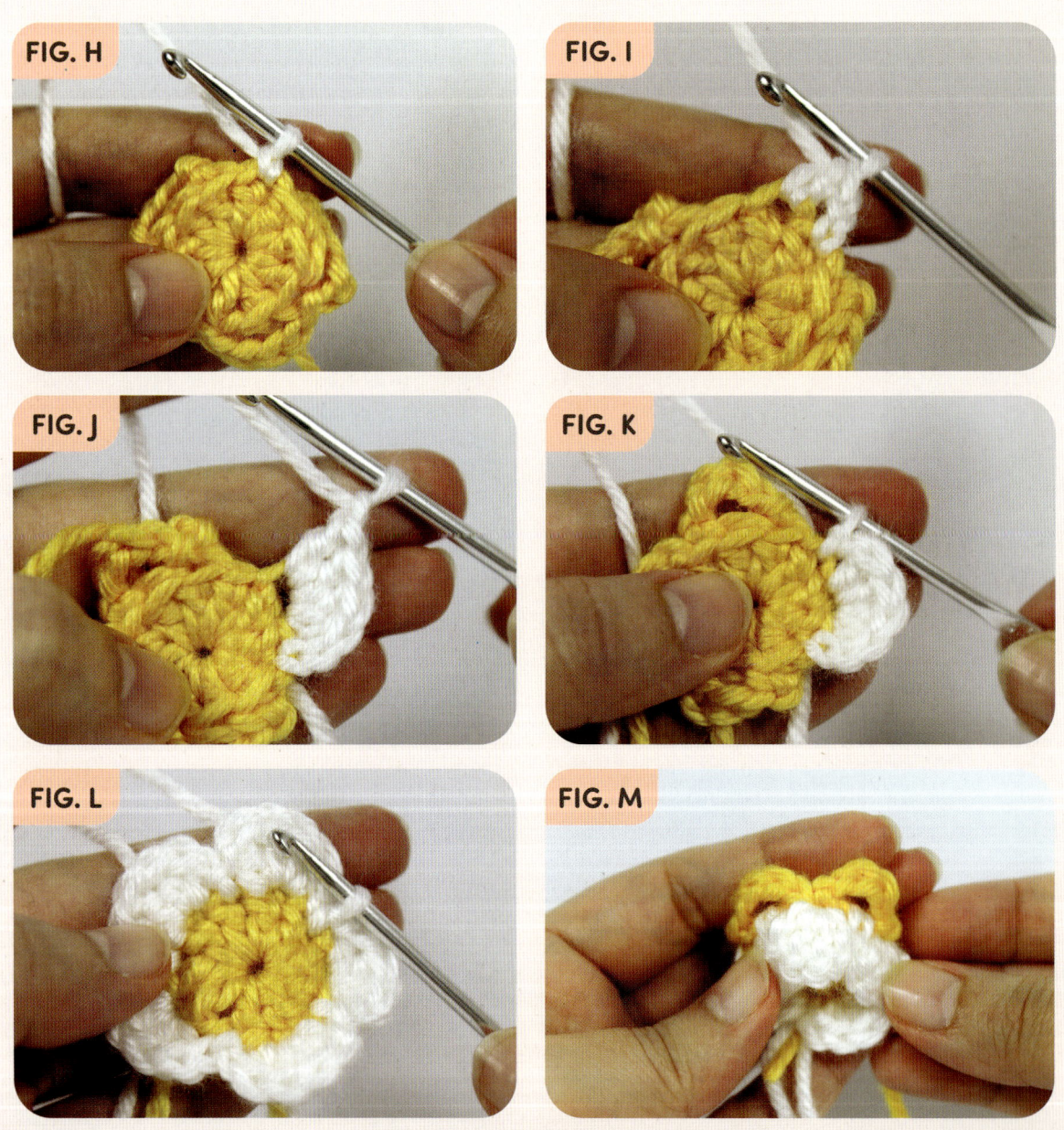

FIG. H

FIG. I

FIG. J

FIG. K

FIG. L

FIG. M

**Rnd 4:** With pink yarn, make a slip knot and, starting in any of the chain spaces **(FIG. N)**, [sc, dc 3, ch 1, tr 1, ch 1, dc 3, sc] into the loop **(FIG. O, P, Q, R, S, T, U)**, repeat 4 times in the remaining loops (5 petals made) **(FIG. V)**

Cut yarn, YO and pull end through the last loop on hook.

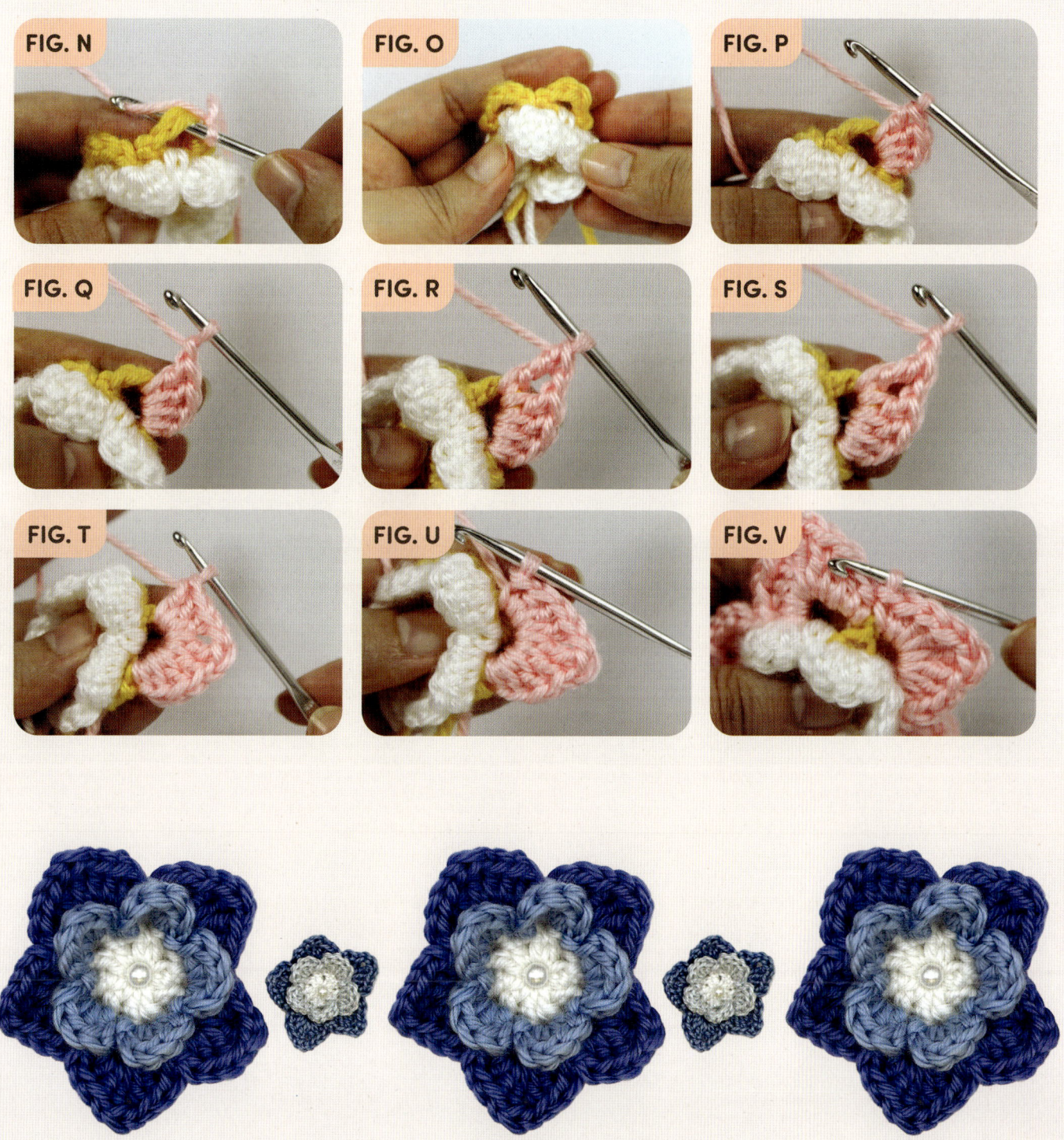

FIG. N    FIG. O    FIG. P    FIG. Q    FIG. R    FIG. S    FIG. T    FIG. U    FIG. V

# 3. Leaf

**Finished size: 1 3/4" long**

Adding a leaf or two to any of the crocheted flower designs gives it a framed, finished look.

**Rnd 1:** With green, make a slip knot and ch 5. Sc in the 2nd ch from hook **(FIG. A)**, 2 dc in each of the next 3 ch **(FIG. B, C)**.

To make the tip of the leaf, ch 2 and sl st in the 2nd ch from hook **(FIG. D, E, F)**.

Work 2 dc into the same ch as the last 2 dc **(FIG. G)**, then continue, working into the free side of the foundation chain: 2 dc in each of the next 2 ch, sc 1 in the next ch **(FIG. H)** (14 st plus leaf tip)

Sl st to the top of the first sc **(FIG. I)**, cut yarn, YO and pull end through the last loop on hook.

# 4. Rose

**Finished size: 2" diameter**

**Row 1:** With pink yarn, make a slip knot. [Ch 5 and dc in the 5th ch from hook] 12 times **(FIG. A, B, C, D)** (12 chain loops made)

FIG. C

FIG. D

FIG. A

FIG. B

**Row 2:** Ch 1. Turn your work so you can work into the chain spaces created in row 1: [sc, dc 6, sc] into each loop **(FIG. E, F, G, H)** (12 petals made)
To finish the last petal, sl st into the chain loop **(FIG. I)**, cut yarn leaving a 12" tail, YO and pull end through the last loop on hook.

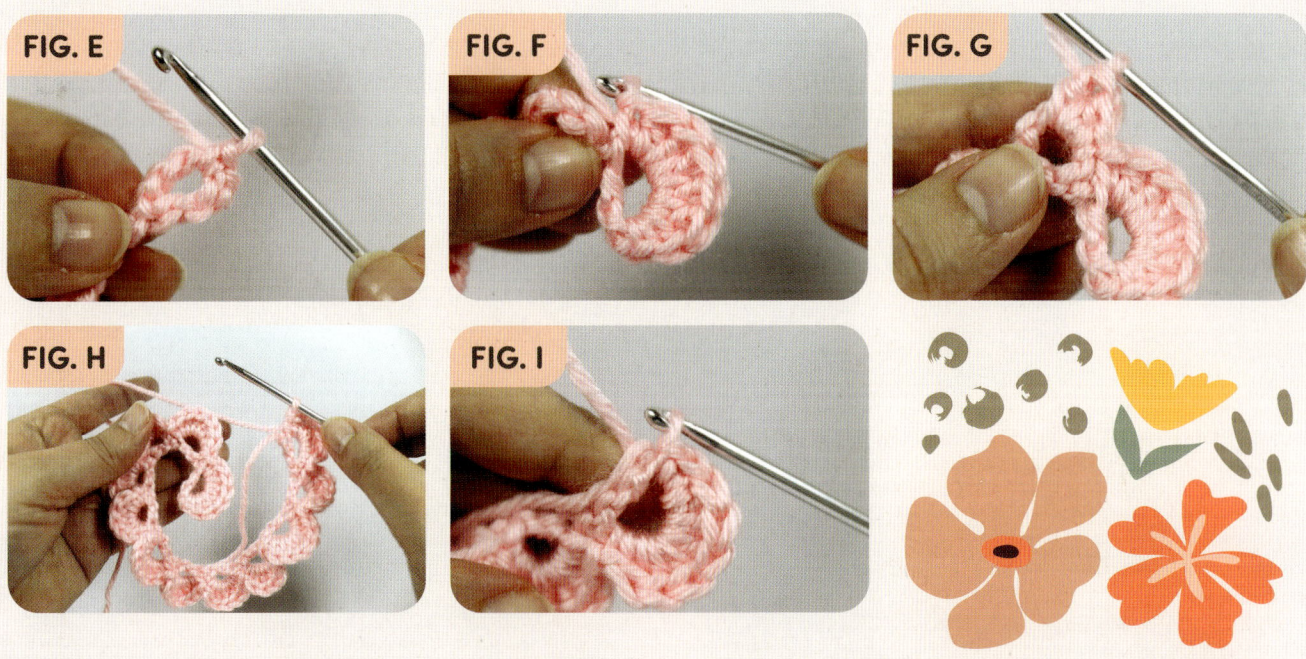

Roll up the piece so it forms a rose **(FIG. J, K)**. Thread the long yarn end into a needle, turn the rose upside down and stitch through the base several times from multiple directions, to secure the shape **(FIG. L)**.

# 5. Four-Leaf Clover

**Finished size: 1 3/4" wide**

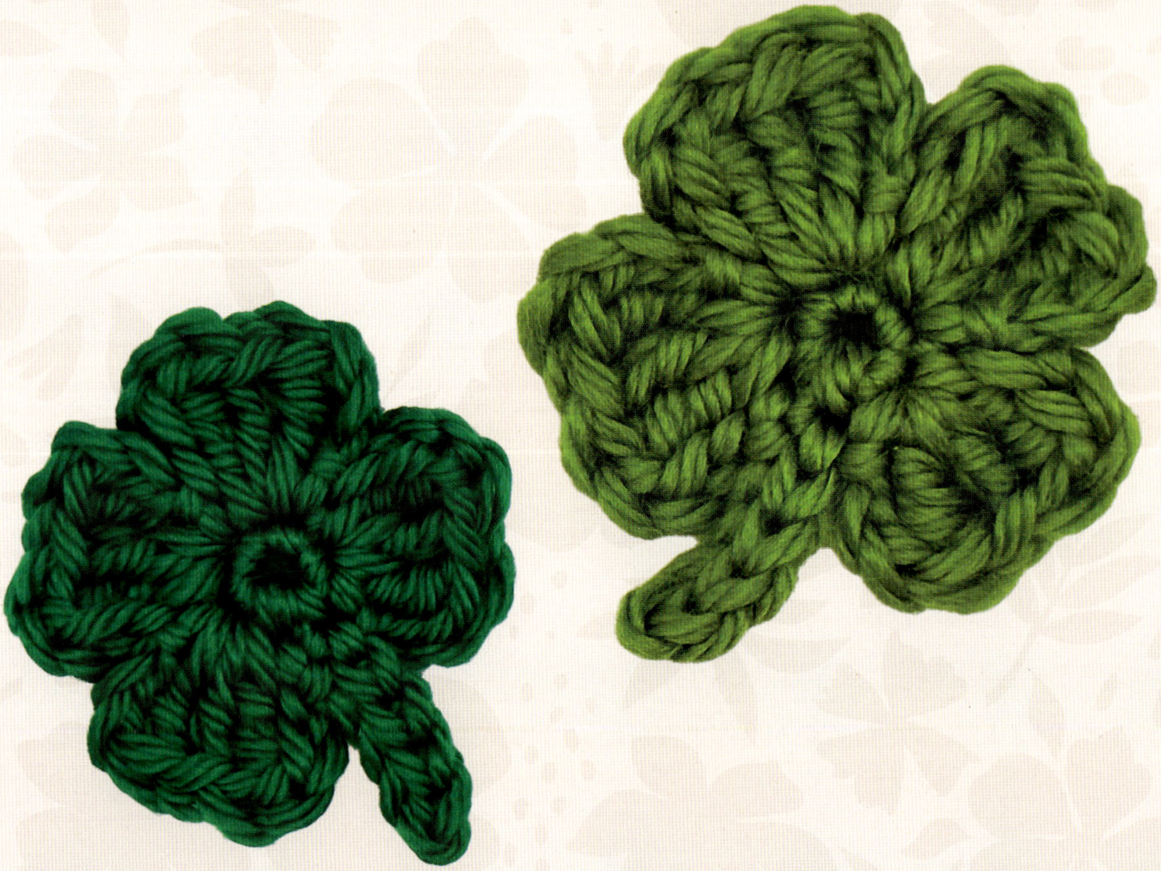

**Rnd 1:** With green, make a slip knot. Ch 2, sc in the 2nd ch from hook, sc 4 into the same ch **(FIG. A, B)** (5 sc)

FIG. A

FIG. B

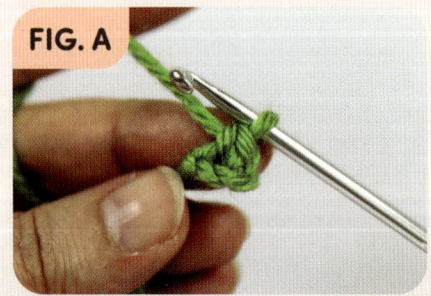

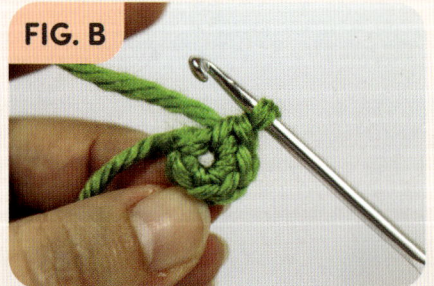

**Rnd 2:** [sl st in next st, ch 3, {tr, dc, tr} in the same st, ch 3] 4 times, sl st in next st **(FIG. C, D, E, F, G, H, I, J)**.

| | | |
|---|---|---|
| **FIG. C** |  **FIG. D** |  **FIG. E** |
|  **FIG. F** |  **FIG. G** |  **FIG. H** |
|  **FIG. I** |  **FIG. J** |  |

Ch 5, sl st in 2nd ch from hook, sl st in next 3 ch **(FIG. K)** (4 leaves and a stem made)
Sl st into the next st (the first sl st of rnd 2) **(FIG. L)**. Cut the yarn and pull on the last loop until you draw the end through. Bring the yarn end to the back through the same st **(FIG. M)**.

| | | |
|---|---|---|
| **FIG. K** | **FIG. L** | **FIG. M** |

# 6. Pansy
**Finished size: 1 3/4" wide**

**Rnd 1:** With yellow yarn, make a slip knot. Ch 2, sc in the 2nd ch from hook, sc 5 into the same ch **(FIG. A)** (6 sc)

FIG. A

**Rnd 2:** Sl st in next st, ch 2, dc 2 into the same st **(FIG. B, C, D)**. Dc 2 into the next st **(FIG. E)**. Dc 2, ch 2 and sl st into the next st **(FIG. F)**. Ch 2, dc 3 into the next st **(FIG. G)**. Ch 2, sl st into the next st **(FIG. H)**. Ch 2, dc 3 into the next st **(FIG. I)**. Ch 2, sl st into the next st (the first sl st of the round) **(FIG. J)** (3 petals made)

FIG. B

FIG. C

FIG. D

FIG. E

FIG. F

FIG. G

FIG. H

FIG. I

FIG. J

**Rnd 3:** Turn the piece so you can see the back of the flower. Ch 3, sl st into the back of the st between the two smaller petals (**FIG. K, L**), ch 3 and sl st into the back of the st between the next two petals (**FIG. M, N**) (2 chain loops made)

Turn piece. Fold the two small petals down to reveal the chain loops you just made, work the next row into these loops.

FIG. K

FIG. L

FIG. M

FIG. N

**Rnd 4:** Working into the chain space, [ch 2, dc 4, ch 2, sl st] in the first loop (**FIG. O, P, Q**), sl st in the next loop (**FIG. R**), [ch 2, dc 4, ch 2, sl st] in the second loop (**FIG. S**).

Cut yarn, YO and pull the end through the last loop on hook.

FIG. O

FIG. P

FIG. Q

FIG. R

FIG. S

# 7. Columbine

**Finished size: 2 3/4" diameter**

## Long petals

**Rnd 1:** With blue yarn, make a slip knot. Ch 2, sc in the 2nd ch from hook, sc 4 into the same ch **(FIG. A)** (5 sc)

**Rnd 2:** Working in BL this round, 2 sc in each st **(FIG. B)** (10)

In the next round, when working into chains, crochet all st into the back bumps of the chains.

FIG. A

FIG. B

**Rnd 3:** Sl st in next st **(FIG. C)**. [Ch 6, sc in the 3rd ch from hook, sc in next ch, dc in each of the next 2 ch; skip 1 st of rnd 2 and sl st in next st] 5 times **(FIG. D, E, F, G, H)** (5 petals made)

**Rnd 4:** Sl st in each st. When you reach to the tip of a petal, sl st in the top, ch 2, sl st in the same space **(FIG. I, J, K)**, then continue around until you complete the round

Cut the yarn and pull on the last loop until you draw the end through. Bring the yarn end to the back through the same st.

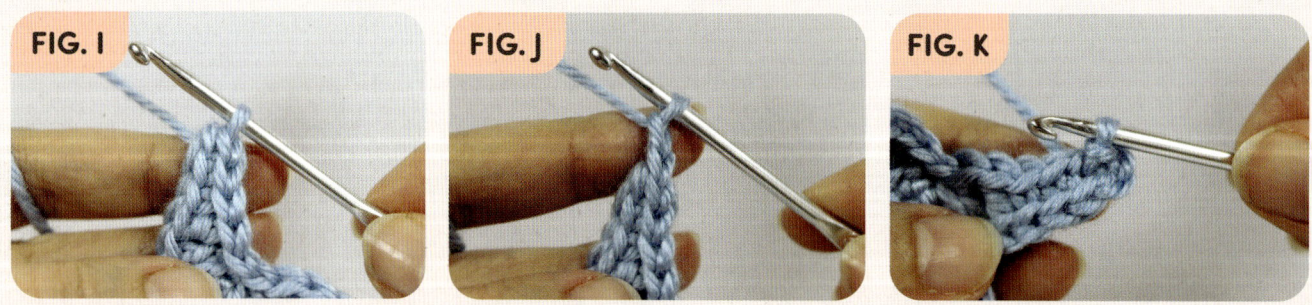

## Small petals

**Rnd 1:** Find the 5 unworked front loops from rnd 2 **(FIG. L)** and work into these. Join white yarn into any FL **(FIG. M, N)**. [Ch 3, sl st in next FL] 5 times **(FIG. O, P)** (5 chain loops made)

**Rnd 2:** Working into the chain spaces, [sc, 3 dc, sc, sl st] into each chain loops **(FIG. Q, R, S)** (5 petals made)

Cut the yarn and pull on the last loop until you draw the end through. Bring the yarn end to the back at the base of the white petal **(FIG. T)**, then do the same with the starting tail.

# 8. Daisy
**Finished size: 2" diameter**

**Rnd 1:** With yellow yarn, make a magic ring, sc 5 into the ring, pull ring tight **(FIG. A, B, C)** (5)

FIG. A

FIG. B

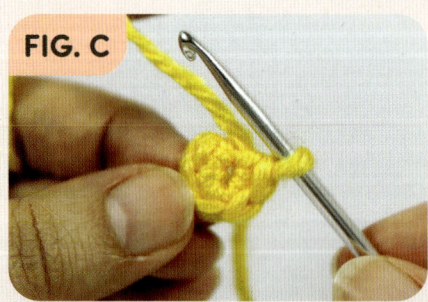

FIG. C

**Rnd 2:** 2 sc into each st **(FIG. D)** (10)

Sl st in next st **(FIG. E)**, cut yarn, YO and pull end through the last loop on hook.

In the next round, when working into chains, crochet all st into the back bumps of the chains **(FIG. F)**.

FIG. D

FIG. E

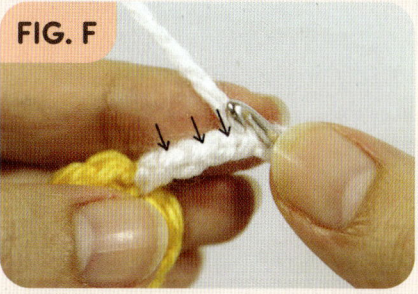
FIG. F

**Rnd 3:** Join white yarn into any st of rnd 2 **(FIG. G)**. [Ch 4, sl st in the 2nd ch from hook, sl st in next 2 ch, sl st in the same sc of rnd 2; ch 4, sl st in the 2nd ch from hook, sl st in next 2 ch, sl st in the next sc of rnd 2] 10 times **(FIG. H, I, J, K, L)** (20 petals made)

Cut the yarn and pull on the last loop until you draw the end through. Bring the yarn end to the back through the same st.

FIG. G

FIG. H

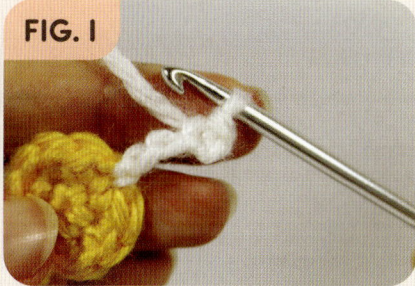
FIG. I

FIG. J

FIG. K

FIG. L

# 9. Sunflower

**Finished size: 3 1/2" diameter**

The sunflower has a doubled center for more stability. If you plan to use it as an applique on clothing, omit the extra layer.

## Center (make 2)

**Rnd 1:** With brown yarn, make a magic ring, sc 6 into the ring **(FIG. A, B)** (6)

**Rnd 2:** 2 sc into each st **(FIG. C)** (12)

**Rnd 3:** [2 sc in next st, sc in next st] 6 times (18)

FIG. A

FIG. B

FIG. C

**Rnd 4:** [sc in each of next 2 st, 2 sc in next st] 6 times (24)

On the first piece, sl st in next st, cut yarn, YO and pull end through the last loop on hook. On the second piece, continue with rnd 5.

**Rnd 5:** Hold the two pieces wrong sides together, and crochet them together by inserting your hook through both layers **(FIG. D)**: [2 sc in next st, sc in each of next 5 st] 4 times (28)

Sl st in next st **(FIG. E)**, cut yarn, YO and pull end through the last loop on hook.

FIG. D

FIG. E

## Petals

**Rnd 1:** Join yellow yarn in any st of the center **(FIG. F)**. Ch 2, dc in the same st, ch 2 and sl st in the 2nd ch from hook, dc in next st of the center, ch 2 and sl st in the same st **(FIG. G, H, I, J, K, L)**. [Sl st in next st of the center, ch 2, dc in the same st, ch 2 and sl st in the 2nd ch from hook, dc in next st of the center, ch 2 and sl st in the same st] 13 times **(FIG. M)** (14 petals made) Cut the yarn and pull on the last loop until you draw the end through. Bring the yarn end to the back through the same st **(FIG. N)**.

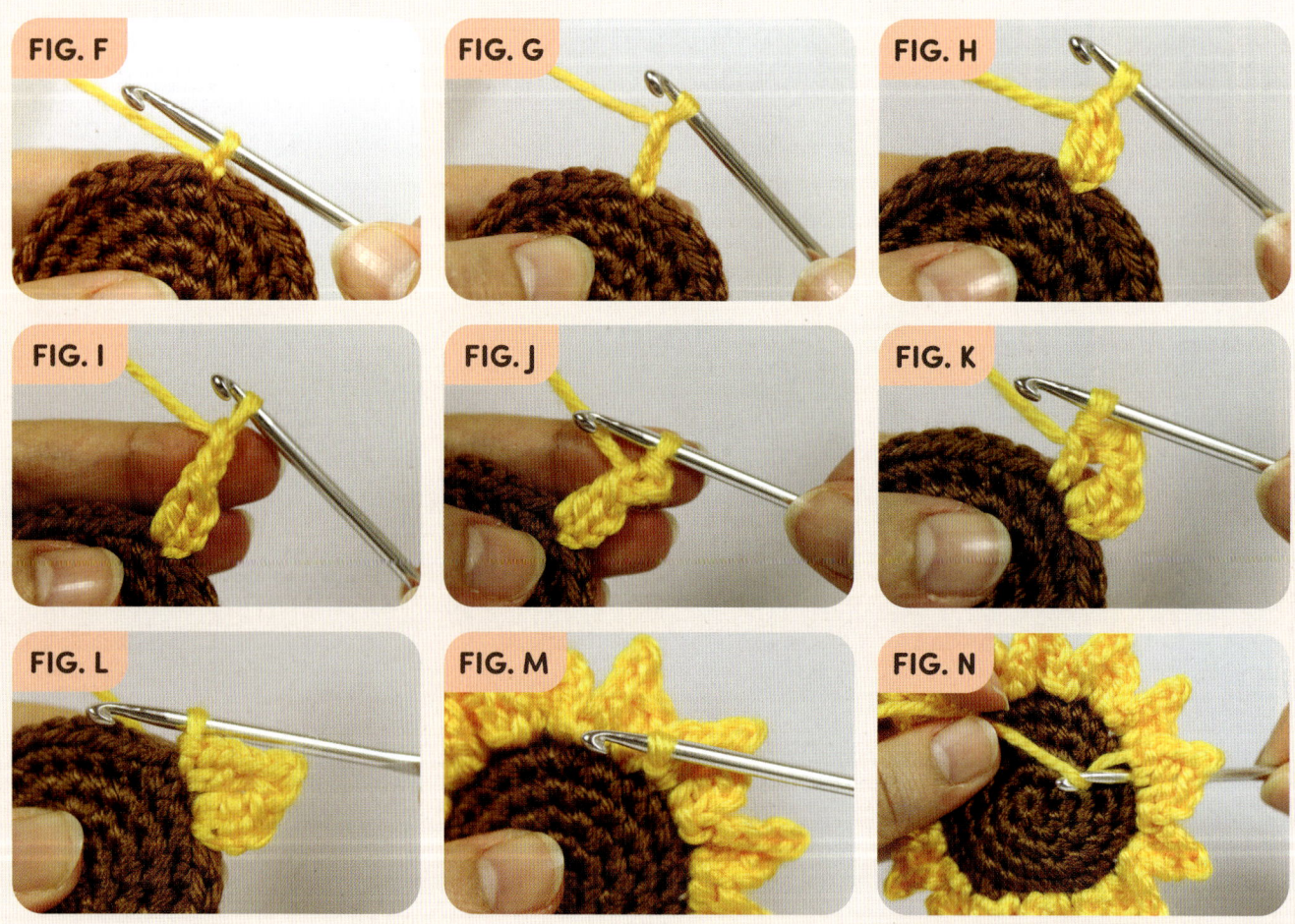

# 10. Poppy
**Finished size: 2 1/4" diameter**

## Petals (make 2)

**Rnd 1:** With black yarn, make a slip knot. Ch 5 and sl st in the 1st ch you made to join the chains in a ring **(FIG. A)**. Sc 10 into the ring (10)

Sl st in next st **(FIG. B)**, cut yarn (leaving a 12" end on one of the pieces), YO and pull the end through the last loop on hook.

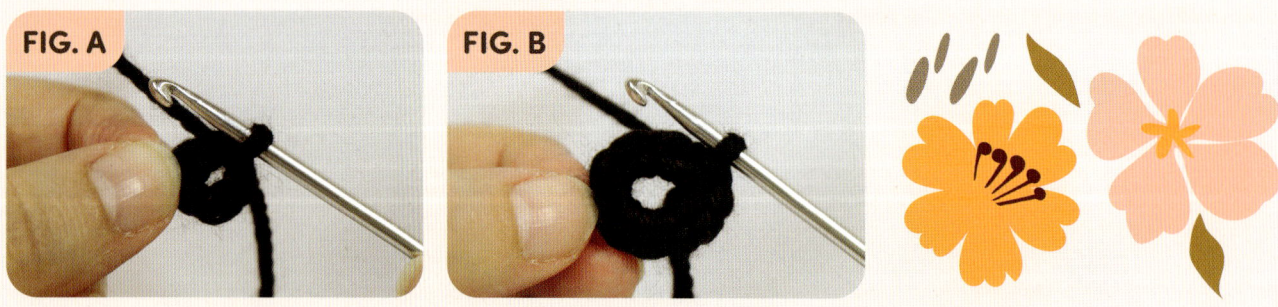

**Rnd 2:** Join red yarn in any st of rnd 1 **(FIG. C)**. Sc and dc in the same st, 2 dc in each of the next 3 st, sc and sl st in the next st **(FIG. D, E, F)**. Sc and dc in the next st, 2 dc in each of the next 3 st, sc and sl st in the next st **(FIG. G)** (20)

**Rnd 3:** [ch 2, dc 1 in each of the next 2 st, 2 dc in each of the next 5 st, dc 1 in each of the next 2 st, ch 2, sl st in next st] two times **(FIG. H, I, J, K, L, M)** (38 st including chains)
Cut the yarn and pull on the last loop until you draw the end through. Bring the yarn end to the back through the same st.

FIG. H

FIG. I

FIG. J

FIG. K

FIG. L

FIG. M

## Center

**Rnd 1:** With green yarn, make a slip knot. Ch 3, dc in the 3rd ch from hook, dc 4 in the same ch **(FIG. N)** (5dc)

Sl st to the top of the first dc **(FIG. O)**. Cut yarn, YO and pull the end through the last loop on hook. This side will be the bottom of the poppy's center—use the yarn ends to sew the opening closed.

FIG. N

FIG. O

## Assembly

Tie together and weave in or cut short the red and black yarn ends, except for the long black tail **(FIG. P)**.

Place the two petal pieces over each other at right angles, and use the black yarn end to sew them together with a few stitches at the border of the black area **(FIG. Q)**. Put the center into the hole in the middle of petals, pulling on the green ends to make it reach the bottom of the flower, then sew it in place **(FIG. R, S)**.

FIG. P

FIG. Q

FIG. R

FIG. S

# Project Ideas

Crochet flowers work up fast, are perfect to use up yarn scraps, and are so colorful and cheery that making them can become almost addictive—but what to do with the finished flowers? Luckily, there are countless possibilities to use them; here are just a few ideas to get you started:

- Customize store bought (or homemade) clothes and accessories with flower appliques
- Sew them on hair clips, barrettes, or headbands
- Attach them to earring findings (available at any local craft store), or turn them into necklace pendants
- Sew them together to make a colorful garland
- Embellish a photo frame with flowers
- Attach them to green chenille stems and make a bouquet
- Use them as the finishing touch of gift wrap
- Create unique gift tags and greeting cards
- Sew together several flowers made from thick cotton for a coaster
- And, of course, make cute botanical brooches! See page 45 for instructions.

# Creating a Floral Brooch

**Finished size: 2 3/4" diameter**

Using your flowers to make a brooch rather than directly sewing them onto clothing has several advantages: you can mix and match brooches and clothing items, you don't have to make sure that the yarn used for the flower has the same washing requirements as the garment, and you can use the brightest colors without worrying about color bleeding.

With bigger flowers, you can directly sew the brooch pin to the back: with sewing needle and two 15" strands of embroidery floss, make a few tiny straight stitches to anchor the floss **(FIG. A)**. Hold the brooch pin to the middle of the flower and stitch through the pin's holes 1 or 2 times to keep it in place **(FIG. B)**.

FIG. A

FIG. B

Then securely fix it to the crochet with multiple stitches across the pin's base **(FIG. C)**. Fasten off the floss with a few tiny straight stitches, and cut off the rest **(FIG. D)**.

If you would like to add a leaf or two, start by sewing it to the flower's back first, then sew on the pin **(FIG. E)**.

If you want to make a cluster of small flowers, you will need a backing piece to hold it all securely together. Crochet a circle with green yarn, following the instructions for rnds 1–3 of the sunflower's center, finish with a sl st and fasten off **(FIG. F)**. Arrange your leaves and flowers on this base **(FIG. G, H)**, then sew them on, first the bottom pieces, then the ones on the top **(FIG. I, J, K)**. Add optional embellishments like beads or knotted flower centers **(FIG. L)**, then sew the brooch pin to the back **(FIG. M, N)**.

**FIG. F**

**FIG. G**

**FIG. H**

**FIG. I**

**FIG. J**

**FIG. K**

**FIG. L**

**FIG. M**

**FIG. N**